THE NO-NONSENSE KEY

Read *Understanding Stock Options and Futures Markets*

- If you want to learn about the hottest financial game in town
- If you want to profit from stock market trends while limiting your risk of loss
- If you want to know about options and futures— the newest stars of the financial markets
- If you want to learn new ways of protecting your investment profits and limiting your losses

D1241748

NO-NONSENSE FINANCIAL GUIDE

UNDERSTANDING STOCK OPTIONS AND FUTURES MARKETS

Phyllis C. Kaufman
& Arnold Corrigan

LONGMEADOW PRESS

This publication is designed to provide accurate and authoritative information with regard to the subject matter covered. It is sold with the understanding that neither the publisher nor the authors are engaged in rendering legal, accounting, or other professional service regarding the subject matter covered. If legal advice or other expert assistance is desired, the services of a competent professional person should be sought.

Understanding Stock Options and Futures Markets

Cover art © 1985 by Longmeadow Press. Design by Adrian Taylor. Production services by William S. Konecky Associates, New York.

Published January 1986 for Longmeadow Press, 201 High Ridge Road, Stamford, Connecticut 06904.

ISBN: 0-681-42111-8

Printed in the United States of America

0 9 8 7 6 5 4 3 2 1

In loving memory of Louis Corrigan

The authors wish to thank John Crowley and Ira Markowitz for their thoughtful comments and advice.

CONTENTS

UNDERSTANDING STOCK OPTIONS AND FUTURES MARKETS

1

THE HOTTEST GAME IN TOWN

The financial markets in the United States constantly change and develop, with new and exciting possibilities arriving in rapid sequence. The last 10 or 15 years have seen the creation of a long and remarkable list of investment choices, including money market funds, tax-exempt funds, IRAs, and asset management accounts, to name a few.

But no other development has blossomed as fast as the boom in trading of *options* and *financial futures*. In a few brief years trading in these new markets has come to rival, in some respects, trading on the New York Stock Exchange itself. The basic financial instruments fueling this growth are *stock index* options and futures—that is, options and futures based on the stock market indexes (often termed the stock market *averages*).

Why? It's not hard to explain. For many years there have been ways in which an investor—or perhaps we'd better say speculator—could speculate on which way the price of an individual stock was going to move. You could easily place a small bet on whether the price of General Motors or IBM stock was going to move up or down. But there wasn't any truly convenient way of speculating on the direction of the whole market. You couldn't easily bet on whether the *averages* were going to move up or down. Trading in the new index options and index futures allows you to do just that, in dozens of different ways.

But speculation isn't the only purpose of the options and futures markets. They are superb inventions for *shifting risks*. While speculators are taking risks in the hope of making a profit, other investors and financial organizations of one type or another are using these same markets to *reduce* their risks. Sometimes the markets bring together two speculators interested in betting on opposite sides of the market. But often a different situation prevails, and a speculator is actually taking on a risk that some other investor or institution wants to avoid.

The institution that wants to shift risk to someone else is called a *hedger*. The hedger is "hedging" an existing investment or other financial commitment by taking on a new commitment that offsets part or all of the risk in the original commitment. In today's volatile markets, with risks that are often hard to foresee or control, many institutions have seized quickly on the new options and futures contracts as a way of hedging the risks in their own giant portfolios of stocks, bonds, and other securities.

So the new options and futures markets perform a vital function, and they have been embraced just as fervently by the risk-avoiders (or hedgers) as by the risk-takers (or speculators). Which is why the volume in these new markets has far surpassed all expectations, and why stock index options and futures have become the hottest game in town.

2

INTRODUCING OPTIONS

Options and futures are quite understandable, but many people, even many experienced investors, aren't clear about what options and futures are and how they work. We'll start by explaining the basics. While options and futures serve some similar purposes, they function quite differently. Let's start with options.

The word "option" means the right to choose, and that's exactly what a financial option is—the right to choose whether or not to buy something within a certain time period and for a specific price. You purchase an option in much the same way that you purchase shares of stock, except that what you buy is not shares in a company, but rather a contract that gives you the *right* and ability to buy or sell something such as securities, stocks or bonds. There are *call options* and *put options*. A call option gives you the right to *buy* something at a specified price for a specified period of time. A put option gives you the right to *sell* something at a specified price for a specified period of time.

Options to buy individual common stocks are among the simplest types of options. Let's say that IBM stock is selling at a price of $125 per share. You can, for example, buy a call option that gives you the right, at any time during the next 3 months, to buy 100 shares of IBM stock at a price of 125 per share.

This call option, or *right to purchase*, has a separate value of its own. To buy the IBM option just described, you might pay a price of $5—which means $5 for each share of IBM covered, or a total of $500 for the option ($5 × 100). Options trade on separate exchanges where their prices are set by supply and demand.

3

The price paid to buy the option is called the *premium*. In this case the premium is $5 on a per share basis, or $500 total.

The price at which the underlying stock can be bought or sold, under the terms of the option, is the *exercise price* or *striking price*. In our example, the exercise price is 125.

Why would you want to buy an IBM call option, and why is it valuable? The beauty of an option is that you buy *a right* to purchase, but *not the obligation* to do so. You have the possibility of a substantial profit should the price of IBM soar, but your risk of loss (should IBM fall, or should you decide not to buy) is limited to the amount you paid for the option. To see how this works out, consider what would happen in the case of our IBM call option.

If IBM stock sells in the market at a price above 125—say at 128—you can buy the stock at 125 by *exercising* your option. You can then hold the stock, if you wish, or you can sell it in the market at 128.

The gain of $3 on the stock (sales price of 128 less cost of 125) isn't enough to offset the $5 per share you paid for the option, and you would be better off if you had bought IBM immediately at 125, or even if you had waited and bought it at 128, rather than buying an option. But what if IBM sells in the market at 135? You can buy IBM at 125 using your option, sell it in the market immediately at 135, and make a profit of $10 per share. After deducting the $5 you paid for the option, you have a net profit of $5 per share.

A $5 profit on an original investment of $5 is a 100% profit. By comparison, if you had bought IBM stock outright at 125 and sold it at 135, you would have had a profit of $10 per share—an 8% profit on your investment of $125. In terms of percentages, there's a big difference. (In all our examples, we are disregarding the cost of commissions in buying and selling both stocks and options. In any real transaction, commissions will reduce your profit or increase your loss.)

What if IBM stock does *not* sell above 125 in the market? If the price of IBM stock declines and sells below 125 during the entire three months of your option, then your option will have no value when it expires. An option to buy a stock at a certain price obviously has no value if the stock can be bought more cheaply in the open market. *But your loss is limited to the amount you paid for the option.* There's no requirement that you exercise the option. If you buy 100 shares of IBM at 125 and the price drops to 105, you have lost $20 per share. But if you bought an IBM call option, your loss is limited to the premium you paid.

Our example highlights two great advantages of options:

First, you have *leverage*. With a relatively small initial investment, you can control a large asset with a large profit potential.

Second, you have *limited risk*. As we've said, your risk of loss in buying an option is limited to the amount you pay for the option. And your risk of having to pay more for a desired stock is limited because your option fixes your right to purchase at a specific dollar amount.

As is obvious from our example, you buy a call option on a stock because you think (or hope) the stock will go up in price. You buy a *put* option on a stock because you think (or hope) the stock will go *down* in price.

Let's say that you had bought a 3-month "IBM 125 put"—a put option giving you the right to *sell* IBM stock at 125. Assume, again, that you paid a premium (option cost) of 5. If IBM drops to 115 in the market, you can buy the stock at 115, exercise your right to sell it at 125 according to the option, and make an immediate 10-point profit. After deducting the premium of 5 paid to acquire the option, you have a net profit of 5. On the other hand, if the market price of IBM stays above 125, the most you can lose, again, is your $5 premium.

These are the most basic ways in which you can use put and call options to speculate on price changes in individual stocks, using a limited investment and large leverage, and with the advantage of limited risk. There are other uses of individual stock options, and we'll say more about the details of option transactions later.

The Trading Markets

One additional point about individual stock options needs to be stressed. They are traded on organized exchanges where you can easily buy or sell through any discount or full-service stockbroker. These include the Chicago Board Options Exchange, and special sections of the American Stock Exchange and other stock exchanges. Moreover, the average premium does not involve a large amount of money. Premiums on options to buy or sell 100 shares of stock usually carry a price in the hundreds of dollars rather than in the thousands—quite often it's less than $100.

These trading exchanges mean that there is a market for options you have purchased and that you can take a profit on an option by *selling* it rather than exercising it. In our example where you bought an IBM 125 call and the price of IBM went to 135, the *market price of the call in the options market* would have risen at least to 10—because anyone could buy the call, use the call to buy IBM at 125, and then sell IBM at 135. In fact, rather than buy IBM with the call, you probably would simply have sold your call option in the market and taken your profit without ever having been required to put up the cash necessary to buy IBM stock.

Or if you became convinced, after buying the call, that IBM stock was not going to rise, and that the price of your option was going to decline toward zero, you could easily have sold the option at any time without waiting for the worst to happen.

So options are liquid—easily converted into cash. But the price will vary, depending on the price of the underlying stock and the supply and demand for the option in the market.

Stock Index Options

If you want to speculate on the price direction of an

individual stock, options obviously can be an attractive way to do it.

What if you want to speculate on the direction of the stock market as a whole?

Professionals generally agree that it's terribly difficult to predict the overall movements of the stock market. But many investors find the patterns of the stock market irresistibly fascinating, and would rather speculate on those movements than on the movements of individual stocks. Besides, runs the argument, the movements of individual stocks often merely reflect the general trend of the market—so why not speculate on the general market trend instead?

Until recent years, it was difficult to find ways to speculate on the general market with the kind of *leverage* that we have seen at work in stock options. But since 1982, two new financial products, *stock index options* and *stock index futures*, have solved this problem and transformed the speculative scene.

We'll discuss these new phenomena in more detail in later chapters. For the moment, we'll simply say that stock index options are a very special kind of option. Because these options are based on the *stock market averages*, you can now speculate on the direction of the market averages with the same advantages found in individual stock options: *low initial investment* and *limited risk*.

Other Roles for Options

One more general word about options. In discussing both individual stock options and stock index options, we have stressed their attractiveness for those who want to speculate directly on the movements of individual stock prices and of the market averages. That is their main interest for many individual investors.

But options are versatile instruments. They can also be used for different kinds of risk-taking operations, some of which we will describe later on.

And since options are a means of *transferring risk*, they can also be used for *reducing risks*. That is true of index options as well as stock options. We'll mention some of these techniques later on as well.

But before we go into more detail on options, we want to introduce you briefly to another fascinating group of instruments—financial futures.

3

INTRODUCING FINANCIAL FUTURES

A future, like an option, is a contract. However, unlike an option contract which gives you the *right*, but not the obligation, to buy or sell a security or other asset, a futures contract gives you the *obligation*.

To understand futures, it helps to know where they came from. Until fairly recently, trading on the futures exchanges was concentrated in real goods or *commodities*—wheat, corn, copper, cotton, pork bellies, and so forth.

For those who sell commodities, such as farmers, and for those who use them, such as canned corn packers, it's good business practice to plan ahead by making commitments today for the *future sale* of the product or the *future purchase* of necessary raw materials. A farmer might contract to sell wheat in units of 1000 bushels at a price that makes for a satisfactory profit months before he harvests and delivers the wheat. That contract is traded as a commodity future. Meanwhile, a large bakery hundreds of miles from the farmer decides to lock in the cost of wheat for the next several months. It goes to the futures market and buys contracts for the wheat at the going price in the market. Neither the farmer nor the baker needs to know each other, and in fact, because so many transactions like this are centralized, each gets a fair price, unaffected by their own local supply and demand conditions. The farmer can sell even before he plants; the baker can lock in a price but not pay until the wheat is delivered. In the meantime, speculators, investors, distributors, and others can trade the contract back and forth, changing the price of the wheat as time passes.

Financial Futures

It was not until the 1970s that someone had the ingenious idea of translating futures trading from commodities to securities. If you can buy wheat, cotton and copper for future delivery, why not stocks and bonds?

And so developed *financial futures*. There are three main types of financial futures: interest rate futures, stock index futures, and currency futures.

Interest Rate Futures

Interest rate futures are so called because they are contracts for future delivery of U.S. Treasury bonds and certain other debt securities. Since prices of bonds and other debt securities fluctuate in response to changes in the level of interest rates, these contracts permit you to speculate or hedge on the future direction of interest rates.

For anyone who follows the debt markets, interest rates, and Federal Reserve policy, this area is an exciting one. For professionals, these contracts have become an immensely popular way of hedging (protecting) against market risks in portfolios of bonds and other debt securities. We'll discuss interest rate futures at greater length in Chapter 13.

Stock Index Futures

The second main type of financial future is *stock index futures*. It took some years before futures trading was extended from *bonds* to *stocks*. The concept of buying a package of stocks for future delivery is not as simple as it may sound. In 1982, however, the first stock index future was introduced—slightly earlier than the first stock index option.

Stock index futures provide a different way of speculating (or of shifting risk) based on the movements of the stock market averages. As with index options, your leverage as a speculator is great. But in contrast to options, there's no premium to pay, and your risk is unlimited.

Other Trading Items

The third main type of financial future, *currency futures*, is outside the scope of this book. But we will introduce you later on to another invention of the futures markets, *options on futures contracts*—a hybrid invention that is different from options on individual stocks or options on stock indexes.

Margin

Certain differences between futures and options need to be stressed. The buyer of an option pays a premium to acquire the option because the option confers a *right*—a right to buy or sell, without an obligation. In a *futures* transaction, neither the buyer nor seller has bought a right—both have incurred an obligation. And since there's no option feature involved, neither side pays a premium. But each side puts up a good faith deposit to guarantee fulfillment of the purchase or sale obligation. This deposit is called *margin*.

Note that margin has different meanings in the stock market and the futures markets. In buying stocks, if you borrow part of the purchase price, margin is the part you put up yourself. In the futures markets, margin is *not* part of the purchase price but is, as we've said, a good faith deposit.

The purpose of this good faith deposit is to cover any losses you may have on the futures contract. If the market goes against you, and your potential loss grows larger, you will be asked to put up more margin, or else to sell out your contract immediately at a loss. Since the initial margin is relatively small (perhaps 5% or 10% of the value of the underlying contract), calls for additional margin can come with staggering speed when the market is going the wrong way.

So it can't too often be stressed that speculating in futures is a very high-risk operation. The amount of money you put up as margin is more, in most cases, than the cost of most options. And, because of the leverage, it's remarkably easy to lose large amounts of money in a relatively short space of time.

Leverage and Hedging

Nevertheless, because of the leverage, the index futures have proved immensely popular with speculators. And here too, as with interest rate futures, the growth of trading has stemmed also from the ability these futures have given professionals to *hedge* effectively. Just as interest rate futures can be used to hedge a portfolio of debt securities, so stock index futures can be used *to hedge holdings of common stocks* against the risks of fluctuation in the general market.

4

A WORD ON MECHANICS

If you're thinking of investing in options and/or futures, where do you begin?

It's important to understand that these two types of investments, though similar, come from different parts of the financial world.

Options have always been related primarily to the securities markets, and the major types of options, including stock index options, are traded, as we have said, on several of the major stock exchanges and on the Chicago Board Options Exchange.

Financial futures, on the other hand, are an outgrowth of the commodity futures exchanges, and are traded on those exchanges (which are now usually termed the "futures exchanges," with the word "commodity" having taken a back seat).

This means that options and futures are often marketed to investors by two different groups of people. The major brokerage firms are usually members of both the securities and futures exchanges, and are glad to handle business in either direction. But many firms deal only in one area or the other. Where there is this separation, the two areas compete with each other. The stockbrokers want to see you deal in options, and the futures brokers want to see you deal in futures.

So when you hear someone praise options as against futures, or futures as against options—make sure you know who is doing the praising, and on what exchanges he or she does business.

Getting Started in Options

Since options require a smaller initial investment and place a limitation on risk, the average investor who has never been involved with either options or futures is likely to experiment first with options. How do you get started?

Getting Started

To deal in options, you will need to act through a stock brokerage firm. You can choose a *discount broker*—a firm that generally charges low commissions but gives no investment advice. Or you can choose a *full-service broker*—a firm that generally charges higher commissions, but which *does* provide investment advice. The choice is up to you. However, if you're just getting started in options, it may be reasonable to pay higher commissions in order to get advice from an experienced broker. (For more information on this choice, see *How to Choose a Discount Stockbroker*.)

Because of the risks involved in options trading, the broker is required to ask you questions about your finances and your investment objectives before letting you open an option account. And before you trade, the broker must provide you with a booklet prepared by the exchanges entitled *Understanding the Risks and Uses of Listed Options*, as well as other information on the detailed rules governing options trading.

The phrase "listed options" is a reminder that these options are traded on organized exchanges, subject to all sorts of rules for investor protection, with prices set freely by supply and demand. These prices are reported daily in leading newspapers (and minute-to-minute on brokers' quotation screens). You have a choice of stock index options and a wide assortment of options on hundreds of different individual stocks; and the exchange mechanism makes it relatively simple to sell an option you have bought when you want to get rid of it—though the sale may involve a profit or loss, depending on the movement of the market.

Are options and/or futures for you? You probably won't be able to answer that question until you know more about how they work. We'll move on shortly to a more detailed discussion of individual stock options. But first, a few special comments about speculation.

5

A WORD ON SPECULATION

Is speculation good or bad? For many people, perhaps most people, the word has a suspicious ring. Since much of this book is about speculation, let us share our viewpoint with you. .

First, speculation does, at least in some areas, serve a necessary purpose. As we pointed out in Chapter 1, the speculator may voluntarily take on a risk which someone else is trying to avoid. In many financial markets, speculation is the oil that makes the machinery run smoothly.

There is always fear, sometimes justified, that speculation might get out of hand and dominate markets that are not supposed to be speculative. Sometimes, at least temporarily, this seems to happen, despite all sorts of rules that have been framed by the exchanges to prevent it. But in the case of the options and futures markets, it appears that the benefits outweigh the occasional distortions. There's no reason to think that the new boom in stock index options and futures is a menace to other financial markets or to the economy.

Are These Markets for You?

Are the markets in options and futures for everyone? Certainly not. Most people of limited means should not be speculating and should only invest in ways that are cautious enough so that they don't need the hedging (that is, risk-reducing) techniques that the options and futures markets provide.

There is no point in denying the wide appeal of the

new markets. Many people start out with a feeling that the entire stock market is inevitably linked to speculation. While investment experts will tell you that long-term investments in common stocks shouldn't be thought of as speculation, many individuals continue to think in terms of "playing the market" or "taking a flyer in the market"—which usually means speculating on how stock prices will move over a short or intermediate period.

Perhaps people shouldn't think in these terms. But since they *do*, at least the new markets have the great merit of letting you speculate precisely and intelligently. You can see your risks clearly, and you can choose techniques that strictly limit them.

Since you know that you are speculating and not investing, you are likely to be more clear-headed than if you were trying to do two things at once. Many investors have bought stocks that turned out to be bad speculations, and then held on to them in the hope that they might turn into good investments. In options and futures, you don't have the opportunity to make that kind of double error. If you're wrong, you're wrong. The discipline may be painful, but it can also be refreshing.

So as to the question of whether or not these markets are for you, there's no simple answer. But in any case, you owe it to yourself to learn about them. If you are an investor, even a conservative one, you need to know about the hedging moves that can be accomplished with options and futures. If you are a noninvestor, you still need to know why these new markets have quickly become leading stars in the financial world.

And if you are a speculator, or have the temperament to be one, then all the more reason to learn how the new games work. Who knows? You might end up finding the *Wall Street Journal* more exciting than the *Daily Racing Form*.

6

INDIVIDUAL STOCK OPTIONS

In this chapter, we'll explain more about how individual stock options work, and some of the many ways in which they can be used.

We've already given, in Chapter 2, an example of a simple option transaction. And we've talked about options giving you the advantage of *leverage*.

An Example of Leverage

Before going farther, let's take another simple example of how leverage works, and why there is a tremendous difference between buying an option on a stock compared with buying the stock itself.

Let's say that XYZ stock is selling at 100 (that is, $100 per share) and you think the price will rise in the next three months. You could, of course, simply buy the stock for 100. (To simplify, we are keeping this example in terms of a single share.) In that case, your risk position is simple. Every time the market price of the stock rises by a dollar, you are a dollar per share richer; and every time it falls by a dollar, you are a dollar per share poorer.

But perhaps you don't have $100 now. Or perhaps you are worried that your judgment may be wrong, and that the stock may fall to 50—a loss you don't want to risk. In either case, you can decide instead to buy a *call option* that gives you the *right* to buy XYZ stock.

Let us repeat that an option is a contract that gives you the right—but not the obligation—to buy or sell a security at a specified price for a specified period of time. A *call* is an option to buy, a *put* is an option to sell.

In our example, the options market would offer you a choice of several call options on XYZ stock, covering different time periods and specifying different purchase prices. Let's say that you buy a "3-month XYZ call"—that is, a call option that gives you the right for 3 months to buy XYZ stock at a price of 100.

As we've said, the prices of options are set by supply and demand in the open market. (While it's an open market, the process is often dominated by professionals, trading according to sophisticated formulas.) A 3-month call option of the type we've described might cost you around $5. This price that you pay to buy an option is called the *premium*. You have paid a premium of $5 for your option.

In the real world, an option covers 100 shares of a given stock. But to keep the figures simple, we'll continue to talk in terms of a single share, with all figures adjusted to a single share.

Look at the table below. It shows what your option will be worth 3 months from now, depending on the market price of XYZ stock at that time (and excluding any commissions).

If you are brilliantly correct and XYZ stock rises in the stock market to a price of 120, your option will be extremely profitable. You can use the option to buy a share of XYZ stock at 100, and you can then resell the stock in the market immediately for 120. You have a profit of 20 on the stock. After deducting the cost of the option (5), your net profit is 15, or a 300% profit on your original investment of 5.

But you don't actually have to go through the mechanics of buying and selling XYZ stock. Since your option can be used to save 20 points on a purchase of XYZ, someone else who actually wants to buy XYZ stock will be glad to purchase your option for 20 in the options market. You have made your net profit simply and with the least possible mechanical fuss.

What if you had bought XYZ stock outright for 100, without paying any option premium? Having

	Buy XYZ Stock at Price of 100		Buy Option* at Price of 5		
Price of XYZ 3 Months Later	Gain (Loss)		Price	Gain (Loss)	
	$	%		$	%
120	20	20	20	15	300
115	15	15	15	10	200
110	10	10	10	5	100
107	7	7	7	2	40
105	5	5	5	0	0
104	4	4	4	(1)	(20)
103	3	3	3	(2)	(40)
102	2	2	2	(3)	(60)
101	1	1	1	(4)	(80)
100	0	0	0	(5)	(100)
99	(1)	(1)	0	(5)	(100)
98	(2)	(2)	0	(5)	(100)
97	(3)	(3)	0	(5)	(100)
96	(4)	(4)	0	(5)	(100)
95	(5)	(5)	0	(5)	(100)
90	(10)	(10)	0	(5)	(100)
85	(15)	(15)	0	(5)	(100)
80	(20)	(20)	0	(5)	(100)

*Buy 3-month call option to buy XYZ stock at 100 (Premium = 5).

saved the premium, you would now have a profit of 20 rather than 15. But a profit of 20 on an investment of 100 is a 20% profit—very far in percentage terms from the 300% profit on the option transaction.

Of course, we've assumed an exceptional rise in XYZ stock. Let's run down the table and see how results compare if XYZ does less brilliantly.

If XYZ reaches 110, your option would be worth 10 in the options market. This would be a 100% profit on the cost of the option, compared with a 10% profit on an outright purchase of XYZ stock.

If XYZ reaches only 105, your option is worth 5, and you have merely broken even on the option transaction. An outright purchase would have done better, giving you a profit of 5%.

Below 105, your option transaction begins to show

a loss. If XYZ stock stays at 100, you would have broken even on a stock purchase, but your call option would have become worthless, and you would have lost your full $5 premium, a loss of 100%. (If XYZ is selling in the open market at 100, no one will pay any price for a piece of paper giving the *right* to buy it at 100.)

But as we assume lower prices for XYZ, a strange thing happens. There's no change in the option results—at any price below 100, the option is valueless and you've lost your $5 premium. But at 95, you've also lost 5 on a direct stock purchase; and at prices below 95, *you would have been better off buying the option.* The *limited risk* feature of the option purchase has come into play, and the fact that you could only lose the price of the option (the premium) has become highly important. Your possible loss on the direct stock purchase is the total price decline in the stock, whatever that might be.

The Option Menu

In the real world, an option gives you the right to buy or sell *100 shares* of a particular stock at a *specified price* for a *specified* time.

As for the time period, listed options are arranged to expire at 3-month intervals, but the cycles vary from stock to stock. Some stocks have options expiring in January, April, July, and December; other have options expiring in February, May, August and November; and still others have options expiring in March, June, September and December. At any given time, options are traded for the nearest three quarters of the cycle. For certain of the most active options, the exchanges have begun to experiment with trading schedules that make options always available for the nearest two calendar months.

In the expiration month, options always stop trading on the third Friday of the month, and actually expire and become invalid on the following day (Saturday).

If it is early January, and PDQ stock is selling around 60, the newspaper listings showing prices of PDQ options on a given day might look something like this:

Listed Options Quotations

Option & NY Close	*Strike Price*	*Calls—Last*			*Puts—Last*		
		Feb	*May*	*Aug*	*Feb*	*May*	*Aug*
PDQ	55	5⅞	6¾	r	1/16	⅜	¾
60½	60	1½	3	3⅞	¾	2	2⅜
60½	65	3/16	1	1 3/16	4¾	5¼	5⅞
60½	70	1/16	½	r	9½	r	r

r = not traded

The table is straightforward enough. The left-hand column shows that the closing price (last trading price of the day) of PDQ stock on the New York Stock Exchange for that day was 60 1/2 ($60.50) per share.

The next column shows that trading includes four sets of options—with exercise prices of 55, 60, 65 or 70.

Finally, the table shows the closing prices (last trading prices of the day)—first for calls, then for puts. The options being traded expire in February, May and August. (Trading in November options will begin only when the February options expire.)

The symbol "r" means that a given option didn't trade on this particular day. For many reasons, some options trade actively while others don't. You should avoid buying an option that doesn't trade in at least moderate volume every day—so that you know you will be able to find a buyer when you are ready to sell.

The option prices are shown on a per share basis. Since each option actually gives you the right to buy or sell 100 shares of PDQ, you multiply by 100 to find the actual dollar cost of the call or put. For example, at the closing price of the day you would have paid 3 to buy a "May call at 60"—a call with an exercise price of 60, expiring in May. Your cost, before commission, would have been $300.00 (100 × $3.00).

How Transactions Work Out

Using this example, the results work out along the same lines as shown in our previous example with XYZ stock. If PDQ sells at 65, your option is worth $500—

because, using the option, you could buy 100 shares of stock at the exercise price of 60 and immediately resell the stock at the market price of 65, for a profit of $500. After deducting the $300 cost of the option, your net profit would be $200.

Example: Rather than use your option to buy PDQ stock, you probably would simply have sold it in the market for a price of 5. Again, your net profit is $200 (sales proceeds of $500, minus cost of $300), which amounts to a 67% profit on your cost of $300.

The *sale* of an option you have previously *bought* is known as a *closing transaction*. It closes out or cancels your position in the option.

Another example: If the price of PDQ reaches 70 rather than 65 before your option expires, your option would then be worth 10 (the market price of 70 less the exercise price of 60). You could sell it for a profit of 7 (market price of 10 minus your cost of 3)—a profit of 233% on your original investment of 3.

If you had bought the stock outright for 60, and it went to 70, you would have had a profit of 10, or 16.7%. And if the stock dropped sharply, you would have lost the full amount of the decline. With the option, your possible loss is limited to the $3 premium you paid, or $300 on 100 shares.

Intrinsic Value and Time Value

We've talked as if options always sold in the market at prices exactly reflecting their value if exercised to buy or sell the underlying common stock. In actuality, options usually sell in the market at higher prices which reflect a whole set of other factors.

The immediate value of an option if exercised is referred to by professionals as *intrinsic value*. An option has intrinsic value if it can immediately be exercised to make a profit in the underlying stock. A call option has intrinsic value if the market price of the underlying stock is *above* the exercise price of the call. A put option has intrinsic value if the market price of the stock is *below* the exercise price of the put.

The difference between the *market value* of an option and its *intrinsic value* is called its *time value,* and might also be called its *speculative value.* Think back to the earlier example. When PDQ stock was selling at 60, we paid a premium of 3 for a May call with an exercise price of 60. The call had no intrinsic value, since the market price was exactly equal to the exercise price. But it was reasonable to pay 3 in the hope that in the months before expiration, the option *might acquire intrinsic value.* Hence the phrase "time value"—the option only has this extra value because of the *time* that will elapse before expiration.

While the *intrinsic value* of an option depends on the relationship between the exercise price of the option and the market value of the underlying stock, the *time value* is set by supply and demand in the market. The time value diminishes as the expiration date comes closer; eventually, if the option has no intrinsic value, it becomes worthless in the market at expiration date. The time value of an option will be greater if the underlying stock is volatile and tends to fluctuate sharply, since then there is more likelihood that the stock will move in a way to add to the intrinsic value of the option.

Time values also depend on the sentiment of the market. If investors are optimistic, they will pay more for call options. If they are pessimistic, they will pay more for put options. People will pay more for call options in a rising market, and more for put options in a declining market.

In and Out of the Money

Among traders, you probably won't hear mention of intrinsic value or time value. Instead, you'll hear that an option is *in-the-money* or *out-of-the-money.*

When an option has intrinsic value, it is in-the-money. It is in-the-money by the amount of the intrinsic value. Example: If General Motors stock is selling at 69, a GM 65 call would be in-the-money by 4. Example: If IBM stock is selling at 129, an IBM 135 put would be in-the-money by 6.

An option is out-of-the-money when the market price of the stock is below the exercise price in the case

24

of a call, or above the exercise price in the case of a put. The option is out-of-the-money by the amount of the difference. Example: If GM stock is selling at 69, a GM 75 call would be out-of-the-money by 6. Example: If IBM stock is selling at 129, an IBM 120 put would be out-of-the-money by 9.

An option is said to be *at-the-money* when the market price of the stock is exactly equal to the exercise price of the option. Example: In our earlier example, when PDQ stock was at 60 and we bought a May 60 call, the call was at-the-money.

Profit without Intrinsic Value

We've talked at several points as if your profit on buying a call depended only on the intrinsic value of the call at the expiration date. That's not true, since you can sell the call in the market while it still has time value, *before* expiration date. You might do this if the stock has gone up, and the option has risen in price to a point where you don't want to speculate further.

There might also be a price rise in the option based on speculative factors—the option might sell above your cost price whether or not it has gained in intrinsic value. You might possibly make a trading profit in an option that still has no intrinsic value at all.

Increasing Your Leverage

If you think that a stock will have a very sharp move in price, you can increase your leverage by buying an option that is further out-of-the-money. You will pay a smaller premium, which gives you the greater leverage. But your option will end up worthless unless the stock has the sizeable move you are hoping for.

Example: Go back to the table showing listed options quotations for PDQ. Instead of buying a PDQ May 60 call at 3, you could have bought a May 65 call at 1—or perhaps several of them. If PDQ stock went to 70, each of your calls would be worth 5—a profit of 4, or *400%*. But if PDQ stock never reached 65, your calls would end up worthless.

More on Buying Calls

We've now covered enough of the basics so that you should be clear about the chief ways you can benefit by buying calls. The first benefit, as we've said more than once, is _leverage_—the ability to make a large profit on a small investment.

The second benefit is _limited risk._ This may sound strange in a situation where you can lose 100% of your investment; but your investment is a relatively small one.

You can use calls to limit risk even if you have plenty of cash available and don't need the leverage. Rather than buy a portfolio of common stocks, some investors put a limited dollar amount into call options, and put the rest of their money into interest-bearing securities such as bonds or Treasury bills. If the cost of the options is held to about 10% of the portfolio annually, the interest on the bonds or bills will cover all or most of the cost of the options. If stocks generally rise in price, it's hoped that the options will provide as much appreciation as would have been realized on a full portfolio of stocks. If stocks decline, the loss in the portfolio is limited to the cost of the options.

You can also use call options to limit the amount you will have to pay for a desired stock because your option fixes your right to purchase at a specific dollar amount. This could be especially advantageous in a situation where you expect to have cash to invest at some future date, but want to be able to buy stocks at today's prices. By buying in-the-money calls, you can benefit from any appreciation in the stocks until your ship comes in.

There are also more sophisticated techniques of using calls, which we won't try to deal with here. If you are an experienced investor who sometimes sells stocks short (that is, sells borrowed stock in the hope of benefitting from a price decline in the stock), buying a call option is a way of limiting your loss if the price of the stock goes up instead of down. If you want to explore more sophisticated uses of options, plentiful information is available through brokers or from the various options exchanges.

26

Buying Puts

Buying put options is in many respects the opposite counterpart to buying call options. If you think that the price of a stock is likely to decline, buying a put option gives you the opportunity to profit from the decline with limited capital, and with your risk limited to the cost of the option.

Example: Let's go back to the case of PDQ stock. If you expected the price of PDQ stock to drop rather than rise, you could buy a PDQ May 60 put at a premium (option price) of 2. For a dollar cost of $200, you would have bought the right to sell 100 shares of PDQ at a price of 60 at any time until the third Friday in May.

If the price of PDQ stays at 60 or above, your option will expire worthless. But if PDQ drops to 55, your option will be worth 5—a profit of 3, or 150%. If PDQ drops to 50, your option will be worth 10—a profit of 8, or 400%.

Example: Just as in the case of buying calls, you might decide to speculate on a big drop in the price of PDQ by buying a put that is further out-of-the-money. In this case, you could buy a May 55 put for a price of only 3/8. If PDQ stock fails to go below 55, your option ends up worthless. But because you have paid a premium of only 3/8, the leverage works dramatically for you at prices below 55:

Price of PDQ stock	Value of Option	Your Profit	
		Points	%
55	0	0	0
54	1	5/8	167
53	2	1 5/8	433
52	3	2 5/8	700
51	4	3 5/8	967

In gambling terms, it's a very long shot; but in the rare cases when this kind of purchase works, the percentage payoff is dramatic.

As with calls, the *limited-risk* aspect of puts is very important. Before the days of listed options, the only practical way to bet that a stock would go down in price was to *sell short*. In selling short, you *borrow* the stock and sell it. If the price goes down, you buy back the stock at a cheaper price, deliver it to repay your loan, and you have made a profit on the difference between your purchase price and the price at which you sold short. But your risk is unlimited. If the stock goes *up*, you will eventually have to buy it back to repay your loan, no matter how high it has risen.

Short selling remains an important technique for experts, but it's an easy way for the inexperienced to get burned. In buying a put, you may well lose the price of the put, but that is all you lose.

Other Uses of Puts

You may also buy a put as a protective device rather than as a speculation. If you want to be able to profit from a price rise in a stock you own, but want to be protected against severe loss in the stock, you can buy a put. Let's assume that you *already own* PDQ stock in our example of listed options quotations. You are hoping for a good gain, but are also afraid of a loss, so you buy a May 60 put for a premium of 2. You will profit from any rise in the stock, having lost only the premium of 2. And until the option expires, no matter how low the stock drops in the market, the put gives you the right to sell it at 60.

Tax Ramifications

This technique has to be used carefully, for tax reasons. You must own a stock for more than 6 months if you want your profit on the stock to be taxed at the favorable rates on long-term capital gains. If you have owned the stock for 6 months or less, the purchase of a put on the stock ordinarily cuts short your holding period for tax purposes and causes any gain on the stock to be regarded as short-term.

So seek good tax advice before using this technique. But as we will see in later chapters, you can use stock *index options* or stock *index futures* to protect yourself against a decline in the general stock market, without any such tax problems.

When to Sell

We've warned at several points that an option you have bought may become worthless at expiration.

In fact, that's what happens to a high percentage of all options—both calls and puts. When you buy an option for speculative purposes, you are hoping for a substantial movement in the price of the underlying stock. In a large proportion of cases, that doesn't happen. The odds are usually against your making a profit. The attraction is that if you *do* make a profit, it is likely to be sizeable in percentage terms, and occasionally spectacular.

When you buy an option for speculative reasons, and it seems destined to expire worthless, remember that you don't have to hold it to the bitter end. Unless an option is hopelessly out-of-the-money, it may retain some appreciable speculative value (that is, time value) in the market until around the last month before the expiration date. Then the time value shrinks rapidly toward zero. This pattern isn't accidental—it reflects the way the mathematic works out in the valuation formulas used by the professionals.

So if your option is heading toward worthless oblivion, considering whether it's worth salvaging some value by selling 3 to 6 weeks before expiration. (In calculating what you will salvage, remember to deduct the sales commission.) Of course, if the stock suddenly moves sharply in your favor after you sell the option, you will have lost the opportunity to profit. But often that isn't a realistic hope.

As we've said earlier, option prices don't move strictly in line with the price of the underlying stock—they have their own speculative price movements. So if you have a position in options, it's important to watch not only the price of the stock, but also the price of the option.

Exercise or Sell?

If you own an option that is in-the-money as expiration date approaches, you will have to decide whether to exercise the option or to sell it in the market. If your purpose has been simply to speculate in the option, you will probably sell it—only a minority of options are actually exercised.

But you may be in the position of actually wanting to buy the stock, if you own a call option; or of wanting to sell the stock, if you own a put option. Tax factors need to be considered as well as market factors. Each case is different, but an experienced broker may give you useful advice, and you should consider talking to an accountant in order to be clear as to what the tax consequences are one way and the other.

7

WRITING CALLS AND PUTS

In the last chapter we talked about *buying* call and put options on individual stocks. What about *selling* them?

First, a distinction. We have said that *selling* an option you previously *bought* cancels your position and is known as a *closing transaction*. Now we are discussing a different situation, where your original transaction is a sale rather than a purchase.

In this case, you are in effect *creating a new option*. And while the buyer of an option pays a premium in order to acquire a *right*, the original seller, in return for receiving the premium, takes on an *obligation*. If the option is exercised, which may happen at the discretion of the option buyer, the seller is *required* either to buy the underlying stock (in the case of a put) or to sell the underlying stock (in the case of a call).

Because the seller of the option is contractually obliged, he or she is said to be the *writer* of the option, and the terms *writing* and *selling* are often used interchangeably in this respect.

You write an option simply by selling the appropriate option in the market. If you don't identify the sale as a closing transaction (see above), then you have written or created a new option—a new obligation, from your standpoint as the writer; a new *right* from the standpoint of the buyer.

Understanding the Odds

The position of an option *writer* is opposite to that of an option *buyer*. Consider briefly what this means.

We've said that an option *buyer*, in a large proportion of cases, sees the option expire worthless. But when the purchase is successful, the profit may be large.

The *writer* faces exactly the opposite odds. The writer writes the option in order to receive a premium. In most cases the option is not exercised, and the writer simply pockets the premium as extra income. But when the market moves sharply against the writer, the losses can be large—unless, as we shall see below, the writer is already covered against such losses.

The odds are such that over the long run, a consistent writer of options is likely to come out ahead. But the risks in certain types of writing transactions are not for the novice. It's an area to approach with care.

Writing Covered Call Options

Having given these warnings, we'll first discuss an operation that is relatively lower-risk. You write a *covered call* when you write a call option *on a stock you already own.* This is *not* basically a speculative operation; it's a relatively conservative technique intended to give you extra income in the form of the option premium.

Your risk is that you lose the chance for additional profit on the stock if the market price of the stock rises above the exercise price of the option you have written. If this happens, you can expect that the option will be exercised and your stock will be bought away from you at the exercise price.

You can avoid losing the stock by buying an offsetting option in the market. This is a closing transaction which cancels your obligation; but you will almost certainly pay more to buy the option back than the premium you originally received, so that you will have a loss on the option transaction. However, you will have preserved your profit in the stock.

If the stock declines in price, the option won't protect you against loss, but the premium you have received will at least partially offset any decline.

Example: You own Exxon stock presently selling around 53 and paying a dividend of 85 cents per share quarterly. You sell (write) a 3-month call at an exercise price of 55 and you receive a market price (premium) of $1. If Exxon stays below 55, the premium becomes extra income to you, and you have more than doubled your income for the quarter.

If Exxon rises above 55, it will be called away from you at 55. Your total sales proceeds will be 56, including the $1 premium you received—and perhaps you are perfectly willing to sell the stock at 56. If Exxon drops sharply, say to 45, the option won't save you from loss on the value of the stock, but at least you have the extra $1.

Selling above the Market

Our last example may have suggested another possible purpose of writing a covered call option. If you *want* to sell a stock you own at a price moderately above the current market, selling a covered call may let you accomplish that and earn the option premium as well.

Example: You own RCA stock, now selling at 43. You don't want to sell it at 43, but you would be willing to sell it at 45. You could, of course, enter an open order with your broker to sell the stock when it reaches 45. But instead, you sell (write) a 3-month RCA 45 call and receive a premium of 2. If RCA is selling above 45 three months from now, your stock will be called and you will realize not 45, but 47 (the price of 45 plus the premium of 2). If RCA fails to rise, you can regard the option premium as a consolation prize.

Since selling calls puts a ceiling on the profit you can make if a stock rises in price, it's the wrong policy to follow at times when you think that the general market, or a particular stock, is likely to show strong gains. But it can be a sensible policy when you think that the market is more likely to go down than up.

Writing Uncovered Calls

Writing uncovered calls—often termed writing *naked* calls—means writing call options against stock you *don't* own. If the market price of the stock rises sharply above the exercise price of the option, and the option is exercised against you, you have to take the loss involved in buying the stock at the higher market price, and selling it at the lower exercise price. Your loss is reduced in this case by the amount of the premium you received. But the loss is still potentially unlimited.

So writing naked calls is correctly regarded as a very risky operation, suitable only for experienced investors with plenty of cash in reserve. If you write a naked call, your broker will require that you deposit a certain amount of cash or securities as *margin*, to ensure that you can fulfill your option commitment. Margin requirements vary from broker to broker, but in any case, if the market goes against you in the option transaction, you will probably be called on to put up additional margin.

Writing Puts

Except in complicated multiple transactions, writing puts is essentially an uncovered or naked procedure. As the writer, you stand ready to buy the given stock at the exercise price, and you will undoubtedly have to buy it if the market price is below the exercise price at expiration date, and you have not canceled your obligation by buying back an equivalent put in the market.

As in writing naked calls, this is generally a risky operation, not recommended to novices. Your broker will require that you post adequate margin, just as in writing naked calls. However, you might choose to write a *cash secured* put. This means that you deposit sufficient cash with the broker to cover the exercise price in full. The risk is then covered in the sense that you won't be called on to put up additional cash; but if the price of the stock declines sharply, you may still be in the uncomfortable position of having to buy the stock at an exercise price well above its going market value.

Example: American Express is selling at 42, and you sell a 4-month put, exercise price 40, for a premium of 1½. If American Express stays above 40, you keep the premium free and clear. But if the stock drops

34

below 40—say to 35—you will have to meet your obligation to buy the stock at 40. Your 5-point loss on the stock is reduced by the premium of $1\frac{1}{2}$ you received. Still, you have lost $3\frac{1}{2}$ points net—more than twice the amount of the premium you received.

Buying below the Market

Just as you can write a call option in the hope of selling a certain stock above the current market, so you can write a put in the hope of buying a stock *below* the current price.

Example: Coca-Cola is selling at 72 and you feel it would be a good buy at 70 or below. You sell a 6-month Coca-Cola 70 put and receive a premium of $2\frac{1}{2}$. If Coca-Cola is selling below 70 at expiration date, your put is exercised and you buy the stock at 70. But your net cost is only $67\frac{1}{2}$, after deducting the premium you received for the put. If Coca-Cola stays above 70, you keep the premium with no other consequences.

Other Options Techniques

There are other, more sophisticated options techniques that we'll only mention briefly. These often involve multiple transactions depending on complicated price relationships, and they are suitable only for the experienced options investor.

In *spreads*, the investor writes an option (either a call, or a put) and simultaneously *buys* an option of the same type (call, or put) on the same stock, but with a different exercise price and/or expiration date. The option he or she has *bought* protects against the unlimited risk in the option *written*—it means that the written option is at least partially covered. Obviously, results will depend on the price relationship between the options as well as on the behavior of the underlying stock.

In a *straddle*, the investor buys both a put and a call on the same stock, with the same exercise price and the same expiration date; or else *writes* both a put and a call with matching specifications. The buyer of a straddle is speculating that the underlying stock will move substantially in some direction; the writer of a straddle is speculating that the underlying stock will not move much. As in single option transactions, the buyer takes a risk that is limited to the premiums paid, while the writer takes on a potentially unlimited risk.

And there are other, yet more complicated techniques. If you enjoy playing with numbers, want to speculate, and have enough capital to work with, the options markets can give you as much opportunity as you could possibly want.

How Options Are Exercised

We have talked about options being *exercised*, without explaining the process. The mechanisms that the industry has worked out are standardized and relatively simple.

The Options Clearing Corporation (OCC), an organization formed by the options exchanges, acts as a clearinghouse for option transactions and requires member brokerage firms to give evidence that they can live up to their financial commitments.

The holder of an option can exercise it at any time from the time it is bought to the last trading day before the option expires.

Usually an option will not be exercised until close to the expiration date, since until then the option has a certain time value, and the holder would ordinarily do better by selling the option in the market than by exercising it. And, as we have said, most options are canceled out by closing transactions in the market rather than ever being exercised. However, if you have written an option that is in-the-money as expiration date approaches, and you do not cancel the option out by buying back an equivalent option in the market, you can expect the option to be exercised against you.

A holder who wants to exercise an option notifies his or her broker, who in turn gives exercise instructions to the OCC. The OCC then assigns the exercise, at random, to one of the brokers listed on the OCC records as representing one or more writers of that particular option.

If the brokerage firm has more than one such writer on its books, it in turn allocates the exercise to one of the writers, either at random or on a first-in, first-out basis. So if you are the writer of an option that is in-the-money as expiration date approaches, remember that the option may be exercised against you at any time (or, to be technical, that an exercise may be *assigned* to you at any time). And you may not even know of the assignment until a day or two after it happens, depending on the speed of communications between your broker and you.

Moral: Make sure that you are dealing with a broker who is prompt, efficient, and helpful. Of course, this is always important; but it's even more important when dealing with options, because of the time deadlines involved.

Above all, keep in mind that as an option writer, you are very much subject to the risk of unexpected market events. Beware of any sudden corporate development, such as a tender offer, which could change the value of the underlying stock dramatically and cause your option to be exercised at a severe loss to you. Even an unexpectedly large dividend on a stock can sometimes present a problem. As an option writer, watch the underlying security carefully and don't underestimate your risks.

8

BETTING ON THE MARKET

Now that you know how stock options work, we can discuss the new type of option that has taken the financial world by storm: options on stock indexes (or *stock index options*, or simply *index options*).

Index options give you the chance to profit from *general stock market movements*. They also give you the opportunity to *protect* against such movements.

Stock index options have been even more popular than anyone expected. In 1983 the Chicago Board Options Exchange registered a first by introducing options based on the "Standard & Poor's 100" stock market index—*S&P 100 index options*. Trading volume in this option has continued to lead the field. In June 1985, trading in S&P 100 index options averaged over 250,000 options daily. With each option covering a package of stocks valued at about $15,000, a day's trading represented options on a total of about *$4 billion* worth of stocks. Not bad for a 2-year-old.

The mechanics of index options are much like the mechanics of individual stock options. But rather than being based on the prices of individual stocks, index options are based on the prices of various stock market indexes.

The market indexes are averages based on prices of anywhere from 20 to over 1,500 stocks. Each index is constructed differently, but they generally try to represent the movement of the market as a whole. We'll describe some of the specific indexes in Chapter 11.

There's one major difference between index options and individual stock options. You can't deliver a piece of a stock market index, and it's hardly practical to deliver a package of 1,500 different stocks. So when index options are exercised, they are settled not by delivery of securities, but by *payment of cash*.

If you exercise an index option, you receive cash based on the *instrinsic value* of the option—which in this case is defined as the difference between the current market value of the index (on the exercise date), and the exercise price of the option.

But here, just as in the case of individual stock options, you are more likely to sell an option in the market than to exercise it. If you sell it while it still has some *time value* left, you will do better than if you exercise it for its intrinsic value only.

Index Options at Work

Example: The S&P 100 index is currently at 182, and you think the stock market is headed upward over the short run. You buy a 2-month 180 call in the options market at a market price (premium) of 5. Here is what your option will be worth at expiration date, depending on the value of the index:

Value of Index	Value of Option	Gain or Loss Points	%
160	0	− 5	−100%
165	0	− 5	−100
170	0	− 5	−100
175	0	− 5	−100
180	0	− 5	−100
185	5	0	0
190	10	+ 5	+100
195	15	+10	+200
200	20	+15	+300

As you can see, the index only needs to rise to 185 for you to break even. At 190, you have made a 100% profit.

But you won't necessarily wait until expiration date. If the index rises to 185 in the first month, your option will retain some time value, and may be selling

39

at 6 rather than at its intrinsic value of 5. If you don't want to take further risks, you can sell the option in the market at 6 for a small profit. Similarly, if the index goes to 190 in a month, your option will probably sell slightly above its intrinsic value of 10, and if you don't want to speculate on a further rise, you can sell out and take your profit immediately.

What do all these figures mean in actual dollars? For an index option, the value of the contract is the value of the index times a certain multiplier, usually 100. For the S&P 100 index option, the multiplier is 100. So a price change of 1 in an option is equivalent to $100, and when the index stands at 180, for example, the whole contract is worth $18,000. When the index reached 190 in our example, your profit of 5 points represented a dollar profit of $500 on your original investment of $500.

(Note: in all examples we have disregarded commissions and other transaction costs, as well as taxes. On a single-option transaction, commissions are likely to be large in percentage terms, and may affect the profit outcome significantly. As the number of options in the transaction increases, commissions take a relatively smaller percentage.)

Example: You are avoiding stocks because you think the market is headed for a sharp drop. However, you'd like to make a profit when that happens, if it's possible to do so without too large a commitment. The S&P 100 index is currently at 182, and after studying the current premiums on various puts, you decide to buy a 5-month 185 put for a premium of 5. If the index rises above 185, you've lost 100% of your premium. But at 180 the option will have an intrinsic value of 5 and you will at least break even, and if the index drops to 175—a decline of 4%, and well within possibility—your option will be worth 10 and you will have made a profit of 100%, plus any time value that the option may carry at that point.

Do we recommend this kind of speculation? Not exactly. Predicting the movements of the stock market is about as difficult as anything we know. But if you like to speculate, the game is honest, the odds are not outlandish, and the long shots do sometimes come in.

9

PROTECTING AGAINST THE MARKET

Earlier in this book, we pointed out that options and futures are instruments for *shifting risk*. And while many people have seized on index options as a way of speculating on the general market, often with limited capital, others find index options just as effective a way of *protecting* against the risks of the general market.

Every investment in common stocks involves risk. Generally the risk can be broken down into two components: the risks that belong to that specific security, and the risk of general market fluctuations.

In Chapter 6, we discussed various ways in which individual stock options can be used to limit risk. But when the risk is a general market risk, an individual option gives imperfect protection. With an index option, on the other hand, you have the possibility of closely controlling the general market risk in an investment situation.

Professional investors often use various mathematical tools to estimate the degree of risk in their portfolios. Index options and futures are becomng increasingly popular as ways of adjusting the risk level to whatever degree an investor wants. You may not have the same professional formulas at hand, but you can use similar approaches to keep your risks at a level that makes you comfortable.

Hedging a Portfolio

Assume that you hold a selection of stocks for long-term growth, or income, or both. The market has had a strong rise, and you are afraid of a temporary decline.

But you don't want to sell your stocks because of the commission costs and possible capital gains taxes.

A solution is to buy index puts, as a form of insurance against a decline. If the market declines as you expect, you can sell the puts at a profit, partly or wholly offsetting the loss of value in your portfolio. If the market holds steady or rises, you lose what you paid for the puts, but presumably you will feel that the cost of the insurance was worthwhile.

Another possibility in such a situation is to sell index *calls*. This may be appropriate if you expect only a small market decline. Instead of incurring a cost by buying an option, you have earned extra income by *writing* an option and receiving the premium.

However, this works only if the market stays in a narrow range. If the market declines sharply, the premium you receive on the calls won't fully offset the decline in the value of your portfolio. And if the market *rises* sharply, your potential loss on the calls is unlimited. It's a technique to be used only with caution.

Separating Out Market Risk

The hedging techniques we just described depend on a temporary market judgment—fear that a short-term market decline will affect a portfolio. But there are certain other risk-avoidance techniques that make options a more or less permanent part of an investment portfolio.

Some investment managers are confident about their own selections of common stocks, but uncomfortable about the risks of the general market. They are willing to take the individual stock risk, but not the market risk. Unfortunately, experience shows that in a market decline, the good, reasonably priced stocks (mine) generally go down along with the bad, overpriced stocks (yours).

Solution: Buy index puts on a regular basis, in whatever quantity seems adequate to protect against the market risk in the portfolio. If the investor is right, and his or her stocks perform better than the general market, this should work out reasonably well. When the market falls, the increase in value of the puts should more than offset the decline in value of the portfolio. When the market rises, the gains in the portfolio will compensate for the cost of the puts.

Calls Instead of Stocks

There's a completely different type of investor who has no interest in stock selection but who wants to participate in the growth of the stock market without risking serious declines. Here, a different options technique is possible.

In this approach, instead of maintaining a portfolio of stocks, most of the investor's cash is invested in Treasury bills or other interest-bearing securities, while a small amount is invested in *index calls*. The fixed-income securities will provide more current income than an equivalent portfolio of common stocks, while the call options should provide gains whenever the market appreciates. When the market declines, the loss is limited to the cost of the calls.

This approach may work particularly well in periods of high interest rates. As we'll see in Chapter 12, a similar technique can be applied using index *futures* rather than index *calls*.

10

MORE ON INDEX OPTIONS

As you can see, index options are an exciting new tool. But they need to be approached with care and respect.

Many of the risks in index options are the same as those in individual stock options. If you are a *buyer* of options, remember that a large proportion of options expire worthless, out-of-the-money. The market will often move against your expectations, or fail to move at all. Many professionals doubt that anyone can consistently predict movements in the general market.

If you are a *writer* of index options, your odds over the long run may be good, but your risk in any single transaction is unlimited if the market goes against you. A helpful factor is that fluctuations in the market indexes are usually more moderate than those in many individual stocks.

If you are an option writer, make sure that you understand your broker's margin requirements, and under what circumstances you will be required to put up additional margin.

If you are using index options to protect against the risks in a stock portfolio, remember that matching the index to the portfolio isn't always easy. Your stocks may be more or less volatile than the index; and take into account also that there are differences among the indexes. The point is not to match dollar against dollar, but rather to try to match *risks*. This may require a larger or smaller position in an option than would be dictated by pure arithmetic.

If you are a writer of index options, a special problem arises because of the cash settlement feature. If you write an *individual stock option* that ends up in-the-money, you don't know on what day it will be exercised, but you do know the exercise price at which you will be required to buy or sell the stock. In an index option, on the other hand, the cash you owe on settlement will vary depending on the price of the index on the exercise date. You may learn on Thursday that an exercise was assigned to you on Wednesday, at Wednesday's closing index value. But if the market has changed on Thursday, any offsetting action you intended to take may be at a less favorable price. This can be a particular problem if you are involved in a spread or in certain other operations involving multiple options.

11

HOW THE INDEXES COMPARE

Just what index options are available? We've talked mainly in terms of the S&P 100 options because, as of mid-1985, the S&P 100 has been accounting for more than 75% of *all* index option volume. But you'll want to know something about the other possibilities.

In this type of trading, popularity tends to feed upon itself. Investors want to deal in contracts that trade actively enough so that buy and sell orders can easily be executed at any time. Several indexes qualify in this respect. And as we'll see in Chapter 12, several of these same indexes are also traded in the futures markets.

Most of these indexes are intended to be accurate measures of the "general stock market." But the approaches aren't the same in all cases, and the results can be different. Here's a run-down on the indexes that are most important for trading purposes:

S&P 100 and S&P 500

The Standard & Poor's 500 stock index, or S&P 500, is probably the index most widely used by professionals as a measure of the total stock market. It is based on the stocks of 500 leading companies, and it is *market weighted*—that is, weighted according to the total market value of each of the 500 stocks. (Total market value of a stock is the market price per share, multiplied by the number of shares outstanding.) So IBM, with a total market value of, say, $75 billion, will affect the index more than 20 or 30 smaller stocks combined. But many experts feel that an index *should* be weighted this way to reflect the market accurately.

The *S&P 100 index* is contructed on similar principles, but using only 100 leading stocks. In performance, it tends to track the S&P 500 quite closely, though not exactly.

For whatever reason, the S&P 100, which leads the pack by far in index *options* trading, has not caught on in the futures market. And the S&P 500, which easily leads the race in index *futures* trading, has not generated any volume in the options market. So you need to be aware of both indexes.

NYSE Composite

The New York Stock Exchange Composite Index is a market-weighted index based on all the stocks on the New York Stock Exchange—now more than 1,500. The inclusion of more companies makes less difference than you might expect. Since the index is market-weighted, it tends to be influenced primarily by the same large companies that dominate the S&P 500 and S&P 100, and all these indexes usually move in closely similar patterns.

The NYSE Composite is popular in both the options and futures markets. In part, this is because of its broad base. But it's also because these particular contracts are constructed with a lower total dollar value, and requiring a smaller investment, than some of the other broad-based indexes.

Major Market Index

To understand the Major Market Index, it's necessary to be acquainted with the Dow Jones Industrial Average.

The famous old "Dow," which goes back nearly 100 years, is an average of 30 prominent "blue-chip" stocks. Note that in the days before computers, an average of 30 stocks was perhaps as much as anyone could quickly calculate at intervals throughout the day. Now, most professionals are likely to focus on the S&P 500 or the NYSE Composite as measures of the broad market. But the Dow retains much of its fascination and popularity.

The Dow isn't traded on the options or futures exchanges. But the Major Market Index has been constructed to move much like the Dow. It's made up of 20 leading stocks, 15 of which are also in the Dow.

Like the Dow, the Major Market Index is not a market-weighted average, but a *price-weighted* average, meaning that the market price of each of the 20 stocks is taken into the calculation without adjustment. The effect of this procedure is that Merck, for example, with a market price of about 115 in August 1985, carried almost four times as much weight in the index as Mobil, with a market price of about 30. There's little logic in this arrangement, except that it made the arithmetic easier in the precomputer days. But if you like to watch the Dow average, and if you want options or futures that track the Dow closely, then the Major Market Index will suit you well.

Value Line Index

Stock index *futures*, which we'll discuss in the next chapter, came into being slightly before stock index *options*, and the very first of all of these products was Value Line index futures, introduced by the Kansas City Board of Trade in early 1982. In 1985, trading in Value Line options also began.

The Value Line index is quite different from those we've mentioned above. It's based on about 1,700 stocks followed by the Value Line advisory service. But it's not market-weighted or price-weighted—every stock has equal weight. The equal weighting means that the Value Line index gives much more weight to smaller companies than in the case of the S&P indexes or the NYSE Composite. And this means, in turn, that the index is more volatile than the other broad-based indexes—it fluctuates more sharply. For a speculator who expects the broad market to move sharply in one direction or another, Value Line futures and options can provide extra leverage (which means, of course, that they also involve extra risk).

Other Indexes

There are other index options and index futures, most of which trade less actively. We'll mention only a few of these.

The American Stock Exchange (Amex) has introduced options based on stock indexes relating to specific industries. Only one of these has caught the public fancy so far: the Amex Computer Technology index option. The Amex also has an Amex Market Value option, based on an index of all stocks (about 800) listed on the Amex.

There's also, as of the date of this writing, a PSE (Pacific Stock Exchange) Technology index option, and a few other special index options that a broker will be glad to tell you about. But before venturing into any of the specialized index options, we strongly suggest that you gain some experience in one or more of the broad index options described above. Any one of them can give you enough potential gain, loss, or protection to keep you satisfied while you are learning the ropes.

12

STOCK INDEX FUTURES

In the financial markets, the spectacular growth of trading in *stock index options* has been matched by equally spectacular growth in trading of *stock index futures* and certain other types of *financial futures*.

We introduced financial futures briefly in Chapter 3. As we said, one of the three main categories of financial futures, currency futures (foreign exchange futures), is outside the scope of this book. As for the other two categories—*stock index futures* and *interest rate futures*—they are certainly not for every investor, but they have become so important that every investor should be acquainted with what they are and how they work.

You may remember what we said earlier about the futures markets. Futures, like options, are a device for transferring risk, but they work differently from options. With an option, the buyer acquires a *right*, and only the writer takes on an *obligation*. With futures, both sides take on an obligation. The underlying asset has actually been sold, but it has been sold for future delivery, and at the time of sale both sides need only put up a good faith deposit (margin) to insure that they will fulfill the contract when it comes due.

How the Contracts Trade

Each *index futures* contract can be considered as representing a proportionate package or "slice" of the stocks in the underlying market index. The market value of these packages is bigger in some contracts, smaller in others. As of mid-1985, the values ranged from roughly

$55,000 for the NYSE Composite futures contract to about $95,000–100,000 for the Value Line contract.

The amount of cash an investor must put up as margin on a contract also varies, ranging from about $3,500 on the NYSE Composite to $6,500 on the Value Line, not counting commissions. But remember that whatever margin you are required to put up on a futures contract, you are liable for any change in the market value of the contract—in this case, the value of the whole package of securities. If your losses begin to eat into the margin you have put up, you will be asked to put up more margin. Moreover, a broker very likely will not take your account unless your investment capital is $20,000 or $25,000 or more—enough for you reasonably to undertake the risks of this kind of operation.

You can put up margin in the form of U.S. Treasury securities rather than cash, so that your deposit will earn interest. And if the market goes in your favor and your account is credited with unrealized gains in excess of the required margin, you can withdraw the excess or use it for additional investments.

Most index futures trade on a cycle with contracts for delivery in March, June, September, and December, and with the two nearest contracts trading actively at any given time. (The pattern varies—see the newspaper or your broker.)

Note that you don't buy or sell an index futures contract at the actual current value of the index, but at a price set by supply and demand in the futures market. If market sentiment is bullish (optimistic), and many investors are demanding to buy index futures, the futures may be priced substantially higher than the current index. Occasionally, when market sentiment is bearish (pessimistic), and many investors want to sell futures, the futures prices may be below the current index. You have to judge whether the price differential, sometimes termed *basis*, works for you or against you, and whether it is reasonable in the given situation.

As with options, the market mechanism permits you to cancel your futures commitment at any time by selling a contract you have bought, or buying back a matching contract to offset one you have sold. Your futures contract is held by the exchange, and not by any individual.

If you hold a contract to expiration date, settlement is in cash, just as with index options, based on the value of the index at that date. If you are *long* a contract (meaning that you have bought a contract), you profit to the extent that the index closed above your purchase price, and you lose to the extent it falls below your purchase price. If you are *short* a contract (meaning that you have sold a contract), you profit by the amount the index closes below your original sales price, or you lose by the amount it closes above your original price.

As with options, most contracts are closed out by offsetting purchases and sales before expiration date. Any speculative difference between the futures price and the actual price of the index has to disappear by expiration date. If, several weeks before expiration date, this speculative difference is in your favor, you should obviously give some thought to closing your commitment without waiting for the last day.

How Much Profit? How Much Loss?

The actual profit and loss figures in futures trading are easily calculated. Each index has a multiplier. The multiplier is the number of dollars by which the value of a contract changes for each one-point change in the index. The total value of a contract is the current index value, times the multiplier.

Example: You are convinced that the general market will go higher in the next several months. The S&P 500 index is at 190, and you buy a futures contract at 193 for delivery 4 months away.

The multiplier on the S&P contract is 500. So your contract represents $95,000 in stocks (190 × $500), and each one-point move in the index equals a gain or loss of $500 per contract. Your broker requires you to put up $6,000 in margin.

After 2 months the index has risen to 195 and your contract is selling for 197. You decide to sell and avoid further risks. On the rise from 193 to 197, you have made a profit of 4 points, or $2,000 (4 × $500)—a 33% profit in 2 months on the margin you put up.

What if the market went down instead of up? If the market value of your contract were to drop 5 points, your broker would probably ask you to put up additional margin.

At that point you might be wise to recognize an adverse trend and sell the contract at a loss. However, if you were to hold on to the bitter end, putting up more margin when required, and if the contract closed with the index at 180, you would lose 13 points or $6,500, more than the amount you originally put up. Unfortunately, a 5% market decline (190 to 180) is always a real possibility. Which is why futures trading should not be undertaken lightly.

Example: You think the market is in for a quick temporary decline, and you would like to bet on your hunch by putting up less than $6,000. The NYSE Composite index is at 108, and you can sell a 1-month futures contract for 109. The multiplier for this contract also is 500, so your basic contract value is $54,000 ($500 × 108). You put up $3,500 in margin.

After a month the contract expires with the index at 105. Your hunch was right. You have made a 4-point profit (109 to 105), or a total of $2,000, on a 3-point decline (108 to 105) in the index.

You recognize, we hope, that you have been lucky, and that you can't expect to guess the short-term market trend consistently. We'll say more on that point later.

Note that in the above examples, we've continued to disregard commission costs. In futures transactions, with sizeable amounts of money involved, the commissions are lower in percentage terms than in small option transactions, and they shouldn't affect the outcome of your transactions in a major way unless you indulge in very rapid in-and-out trading. To go in and out of a single contract, your commissions might typically be from $60 to $80 at a full-service broker, and as low as $25 at a discount firm. Note also that margin requirements vary from broker to broker, and may change at any time, so that the margin requirements in our examples can only serve as rough guidelines.

Hedging with Futures

While the index futures markets may or may not be a wise place for you to *take* risks, there's no doubt that they have rapidly gained favor with institutional and other professional investors as a place to *reduce* risks.

The hedging techniques used with stock index futures resemble in some respects the techniques used with stock index options. But there are differences. In hedging with options, an investor often pays the option premium as a form of insurance to limit risk, while still preserving the possibility of profit. Stock index *futures* are often used to hedge a stock portfolio in a way that eliminates the potential for both profits and losses—but without the payment of any premium.

Example: The manager of a $20 million pension fund portfolio is worried about the short-term market outlook, and would gladly give up the potential for gains for 2 months in order to be protected against possible losses. Selling stocks from the portfolio would be cumbersome and expensive. Volume in the S&P 500 futures contract is such that the pension fund can quite easily go short $20 million worth of futures (about 200 contracts). If the market declines, the gain on the contracts offsets the decline in the portfolio value. The hedge can easily be eliminated when desired by buying back 200 contracts to cancel out those sold.

Example: A large brokerage firm has temporarily taken on a heavy inventory of stocks in its block trading operations. To reduce its risks in the event of a market decline, it goes short (that is, sells) index futures until the inventory is down to normal.

Example: Another brokerage firm decides to keep its trading inventory completely hedged with index futures at all times, eliminating the "market risk."

Futures as a Stock Substitute

Index futures can be used in other protective ways by large portfolios, and sometimes by small ones:

Example: A portfolio manager has extra cash that he or she plans to put into common stocks. But selecting and buying the common stocks will take time. Afraid of being left in the dust by a rising market, the manager buys index futures, and gradually sells the futures as the individual stocks are acquired. If the market rises, gains on the futures will make up for the gains missed on individual stocks.

Example: In a related tactic, a pension fund manager knows that a big contribution will be made to the fund three months in the future. In order not to miss a possible market advance, the manager buys index futures for the portfolio until the additional cash is available.

Note that you might very well adapt these last two tactics for your own use. Index futures can be used to carry you over a period when you have not decided which individual stocks to buy, or when you are expecting cash that is not yet in hand.

Example: The managers of a bank trust department have decided to sell off a very large amount of stocks. Hurrying the sales might depress the market for certain stocks, but waiting involves an undesired market risk. The managers sell index futures immediately, and buy back the futures gradually as individual stocks are liquidated. If the market drops, profits in the futures offset losses on the individual stocks.

An Unlimited Future

The possible variations are endless. In a technique that resembles one we discussed under index options, some managers, rather than holding a portfolio of common stocks, hold most of their assets in Treasury bills or other fixed-income securities, while putting 5% to 10% of the total in index futures. This may work particularly well when interest rates are high, and when there is not a large premium on futures compared with the stock indexes. Some managers shift between futures and individual stocks, buying individual stocks when the premiums on futures are high, and shifting into futures when the premiums are low. And even more complicated techniques are becoming common.

Although activity in index futures is already phenomenal, it seems destined to go higher as more and more large investors learn how to use the various techniques. The activity of the markets, and their ability to handle and absorb large orders, gives institutional investors a flexibility in managing common stock portfolios that never existed before. Whether this will lead to better investment results depends on the managers, and remains to be seen.

For the individual investor, many of the same advantages apply. But this is a high-risk area. It's important to know the risks before you enter, and it's important to take only those risks you can afford.

13

INTEREST RATE FUTURES

Stock index futures have been a brilliant innovation in the financial markets. But the futures contract that leads all others in trading, whether measured by number of contracts or by the underlying dollars involved, is not a stock index future. It's a futures contract in U.S. Treasury bonds.

Surprising? Not when you think about it carefully. In the financial markets, trading in stocks amounts to several billion dollars a day. But it is dwarfed by the trading in *debt* securities—securities representing debt obligations, coming due in anywhere from one day to perhaps 40 years. Banks, corporations, money market funds, insurance companies and other institutions trade debt securities, from very short-term to very long-term, in almost incredible quantities.

Just as the manager of a stock portfolio faces the problem of managing risk, so does the manager of a debt portfolio. By far the greatest risk in the debt markets is the risk of changes in *interest rates*. For many large banks and other institutions, a rather moderate change in interest rates can add or subtract many millions of dollars to or from the market value of the debt securities the institution is holding.

Interest Rates and Prices

In case you aren't clear as to how interest rate changes affect the prices of bonds and other debt securities, we'll explain very briefly. Let's say you buy a 20-year, $1,000 U.S. Treasury bond paying 10% interest. You pay exactly $1,000 for the purchase. However, interest rates rise, and a year later new Treasury bonds are being issued that pay 12% interest. Investors who now can buy new 12% bonds certainly will not pay full value for your 10% bond. So the market price of your bond will decline so that the effective interest rate matches the current rate. You know that the Treasury will pay your bond off in full after 20 years; but if you want to sell the bond now in the market, the price will be less than $1,000, and you will take a loss.

Conversely, if interest rates *drop*, say to 8%, investors will pay a premium for your bond in order to get the advantage of the 10% yield.

The longer-term the bond or other security, the bigger the price swing for a given change in interest rates. A difference of 2% in yield will mean a lot of dollars over 20 years—enough to move the price of your $1,000 bond up now to $1,200, or down to $850. But if the security is coming due in a few months, a 2% difference means very little in dollars, and the price of the debt security will only move slightly above or below $1,000.

It's important to understand that as interest rates *rise*, prices of existing debt securities *decline;* and as interest rates *decline*, prices of existing debt securities *rise*. Sometimes the language of the debt markets is confusing. If you see a phrase such as "Treasury bill market rises," make sure you know just what went up and what went down.

In the last 10 or 15 years, fluctuations in interest rates in the U.S. have become more and more unsettling, and institutions and other participants in the debt markets have felt a tremendous need for protection against the kind of price fluctuations we have described. Interest rate futures and options have arisen as a way of meeting this need. And the markets have mushroomed.

Interest Rate Futures

First, the futures. Interest rate futures resemble stock index futures as far as the basic trading mechanisms are concerned. In a Treasury bond future, for example, the buyer is actually buying, and the seller is actually selling, U.S. Treasury bonds for future delivery. It's an obligation on both sides.

But these are real securities, not indexes. In the minority of cases where a contract is held to expiration date, settlement is not purely in cash (as with a stock index future). Instead, the seller actually delivers Treasury bonds (or whatever other debt security the contract calls for) to the buyer.

And if you are a speculator, your money can disappear just as fast in these markets as in stock index futures. A Treasury bond futures contract represents $100,000 principal value of Treasury bonds. (Since one bond has a principal value of $1,000, the contract is for 100 bonds.) If you buy or sell a contract, your broker might require that you put up $2,000 in margin (as a good faith deposit—just as in index futures). If Treasury bond prices drop from 100 to 98, which means from $1,000 per bond to $980, and if you were the buyer, you have lost your $2,000 ($20 per bond on 100 bonds). The seller's $2,000, on the other hand, has doubled to $4,000.

As you can see, these markets are not for the poor or the faint-hearted. And because they are generally professional markets, the margin required is usually relatively less than for stock index futures. You have even more leverage—which means that the swings in your margin can sometimes be even faster here than in index futures.

The Available Contracts

The leading interest rate futures contracts are in (a) long-term Treasury bonds (T-bonds), (b) 10-year Treasury notes, and (c) 3-month Treasury bills (T-bills). Treasury bills, being very short-term, don't fluctuate very much in price; but since in this case each contract covers *$1,000,000* in bills (not $100,000), the extra leverage produces plenty of action.

Expiration months are March, June, September, and December. At any given time, you can trade futures for delivery as much as a year or more away (more than 2 years in the case of T-bonds). So, with these three contracts, you can speculate or hedge in long-term, intermediate-term, or short-term interest rates; and you can focus on the level of those rates as much as 2 years in the future.

There are also futures contracts (generally less active) on certain other types of debt instruments—including GNMA (Ginnie Mae) mortgage participation certificates, bank CDs (certificates of deposit), and most recently a contract based on an index of municipal bond prices.

How Institutions Hedge

We doubt that interest rate futures are suitable for most individual investors. So rather than go into details of pricing and trading, we'll outline some of the ways in which investment professionals have put these contracts to work in tremendous volume.

The professionals, of course, are generally interested in protection rather than speculation. The simplest and perhaps most welcome feature of debt futures is that they make it possible to hedge a portfolio of bonds or other debt securities against interest rate risks.

Dealers in Treasury securities, who handle Treasury securities in the billions of dollars, are among the major hedgers. By selling (going short) futures contracts, they can offset part or all of their interest rate risks. If interest rates rise, and bond prices decline, the profit on the futures contracts can offset the loss in their actual bond inventory.

In exactly the same way, a pension fund that holds T-bonds as an investment for income can hedge against price declines in the bonds by going short T-bond futures.

In hedging against loss, the government dealers and the pension fund also give up the opportunity for an interest rate profit. If rates decline, and bond prices rise, the losses they suffer on their short futures positions will offset the profits on bonds that they hold. But that is the nature of this type of hedging. The

60

dealers are holding bonds for trading inventory, and the pension fund is holding bonds for income; both are glad to forgo interest rate *profits* if they can be shielded against interest rate *losses*.

Comparing Futures and Options

In either case, as we shall see in Chapter 15, it would be possible to hedge with interest rate *options* instead of futures. By buying puts instead of selling futures, the dealer or pension fund could protect against loss while at the same time retaining the possibility of a profit. Why futures instead of options? In using options, the institution would be *risking* the option premium in order to retain the possibility of a profit. The risk would be limited, but it would still be a risk. If the dealer, bank, institution, etc. wants to eliminate interest rate risk completely and neutralize its portfolio, futures are a better choice.

Some Other Possibilities

Some other possible uses of debt futures resemble techniques that we saw used in stock futures. A pension fund may expect a company contribution 3 months from now that it plans to put into T-bonds. Rather than risk a decline in interest rates, the fund *buys* T-bond futures now. If rates decline, the profit on the futures will offset the lower income that will be obtained when the money is available.

A different example: A corporation plans to raise cash in a few months by selling bonds to the public. Interest rates now are favorably low to the corporation, which protects itself by *selling* T-bond futures. If interest rates rise, and bond prices fall, the corporation will have a profit on the T-bond futures that will partly or wholly offset the higher interest rate it will have to pay on its bond issue.

There are many other, more complicated hedging techniques that are regularly used in the interest rate futures markets. Professional traders move in and out of the markets, taking advantage of slight differences between prices of futures and prices of actual bonds, notes and other debt securities. This "arbitrage" process keeps the markets active and efficient both for the speculator and the hedger.

We've said that the options and futures markets have the function of *transferring risk*. If you want to see this process at work on a grand scale, it's hard to find a better subject than the interest rate futures markets.

Is There a Future in Your Mortgage?

Are interest rate futures for you? If you are a large investor, the answer may well be yes. For the smaller investor, it's not so clear.

As we've seen, these markets let you speculate on the future direction of interest rates. The minimum amounts are large, and the risks are very high. Interest rates are notoriously hard to predict; and this can be a dangerous area both for the professional and the amateur.

Can you use these markets for protection? Not easily, but there's one area that might be worth considering in special circumstances. The biggest debt transaction in the lives of many people is the taking on and paying off of a home mortgage. It's possible to imagine certain circumstances where debt futures could help you handle the interest rate risk in a home mortgage:

Example: You expect to be shopping for a home a year from now. Interest rates are low now, and you are afraid they will rise. You sell a T-bond future, or, better yet, a Ginnie Mae future (which is based on mortgage rates). If interest rates rise, and prices of existing bonds and mortgages decline, you will have a profit on your futures contract that may compensate for the higher interest rate you will have to pay when you are ready to take out a mortgage loan.

Example: You expect to sell your house in a year and invest the cash. Interest rates are high now, but you are afraid they will fall. In the reverse of the above example, you *buy* a T-bond or Ginnie Mae future. If interest rates decline, the profit on your futures contract will compensate for the lower interest you will earn on your cash when the house is sold.

Example: You have a large adjustable rate mortgage on your home. You are afraid that rates will rise and your mortgage payments will increase. You sell a futures contract. If rates rise, the profit on your contract will offset the pain of higher mortgage payments.

Obviously, it would not be easy to match a futures contract exactly against the interest rate risk involved in your mortgage. And if interest rates go contrary to your expectations, you could have a large loss on your futures contract. But the examples will show you that in an economy where borrowing and lending are universal activities, interest rate futures can have surprising applications.

14

WHY OPTIONS ON FUTURES?

Options on futures—isn't that carrying the whole game a little too far?

Futures options, as they are called, were introduced in 1982 and have become a respectable part of the financial scene, though they don't begin to match the trading volume of stock index options or debt futures.

A futures option is actually an option to buy or sell a particular futures contract. If the option is exercised, settlement is not in cash (as with a stock index option) but through actual delivery of a futures contract. Since futures contracts generally represent a large dollar value, these options come in much larger units than the various options discussed in earlier chapters. Premiums on at-the-money options are likely to run in the $1,000–$3,000 range. And just as with smaller options, it's remarkably easy to lose your whole premium.

Why Futures Options?

There are a few reasons for the existence of futures options. One is simply competition among the trading exchanges. Options, which are traded on the stock exchanges and the Chicago Board Options Exchange, have been a great success. It's natural for the futures exchanges to want a piece of this very good business. Futures options have given them a piece of the pie.

From a trading standpoint, the results have been mixed. Options on interest rate futures, for reasons we will see shortly, have been a substantial success. Options on stock index futures, on the other hand, have done respectably but not brilliantly.

Stock Index Futures Options

Options on stock index *futures* are the futures exchanges' own variation on stock index options (see Chapters 8–11). For the sophisticated investor, they offer the opportunity to play two differentials at once: the relation of the stock index futures contract to the stock index itself, and the relation of the option to the futures contract. Since the futures contracts are more volatile (that is, fluctuate more sharply) than the underlying stock indexes, the futures options also may swing more sharply than ordinary index options.

The average investor doesn't need the extra complication or the extra volatility. We suggest that until you get quite expert in stock index options, the futures options are better left alone.

If you do become expert, there are options on both the S&P 500 index futures and the NYSE Composite index futures. It's worth noting that the dollar value of the NYSE futures option is only about half that of the S&P 500.

Trading and hedging techniques with these options resemble those previously discussed for ordinary stock index options, with the extra complication of relating transactions to the variations of the futures contracts as well as the movements of the index itself. As we've said, for the average investor it doesn't appear that these options add significantly to the possibilities of index options, and the index options come in smaller, more manageable units.

Options on interest rate futures, on the other hand, play a very specific role that isn't easily filled elsewhere. More on that in the next chapter.

15

INTEREST RATE FUTURES OPTIONS

To repeat our earlier question—why options on futures? In the case of options on interest rate futures, the reasons are convincing.

Options exist on certain *specific* debt securities, but they have not been a great success. There are options on a few different Treasury bond and note issues. But from the standpoint of options traders and hedgers, these have shortcomings. First, each option is tied to a specific bond or note issue and calls for delivery of that particular issue. This limits the flexibility of the option.

Second, it's hard to pinpoint the current market price of a bond or note. Treasury bonds and notes are traded in a vast *over-the-counter* network of dealers, banks and other financial institutions. At any given time, four dealers might quote four slightly different prices for the same bond or note issue. So traders and hedgers in these options lack a precise base on which they can calculate premiums and complicated value relationships.

The solution: futures options. Interest rate futures trade on exchanges where prices are precisely known from minute to minute. They are not tied to any one note or bond issue. They offer a perfect base for options trading.

There are options on Treasury *bond* futures and options on Treasury *note* futures. The T-bond option has been the winner, trading in a volume probably second only to the S&P 100 index option.

You can speculate on interest rate movements by outright option purchases. You can buy a call if you expect a rise in bond prices (and a decline in interest rates). You can buy a put if you expect a decline in bond prices (and a rise in interest rates). Although your option relates to the futures contract, it is much as though you had an option on a direct debt security.

For hedging purposes, banks, Treasury dealers, and others involved with debt securities can use T-bond futures *options* to hedge much as they can use T-bond *futures* (see Chapter 13). A portfolio of debt securities can be hedged against price declines by buying puts. And most other hedging techniques can be translated into option terms. As we've pointed out, by using options and paying a premium, it's possible to hedge against loss while still preserving the possibility of a profit.

The options also allow you to hedge against a futures position. Let's say you are convinced interest rates are going down, you have enough capital for speculation, but you want to limit your losses. You could buy a T-bond future and at the same time buy a T-bond put with an exercise price somewhat below the market. If, contrary to your hope, interest rates rise and your T-bond future falls, you can use the put to sell the contract at the exercise price and limit your loss. If interest rates decline as you expected, the profit on your futures contract is unlimited, except that you must deduct the "insurance premium" you paid to purchase the put.

If you want to speculate on interest rate movements while limiting your potential loss to an option premium, interest rate options obviously give you a way to do it. But we repeat that the premiums are large. On a typical day in August 1985, the December 1985 T-bond *futures* contract was trading at a price of around 76, representing a market value of about $76,000 per contract of 100 bonds. A 3-month call *option* (option to buy) on that contract at 76 would have cost you close to $1,900. And remember how easy it is for an option premium to become completely worthless.

So proceed with caution—lots of caution.

16

A TAX BREAK WORTH CONSIDERING

Up until now, we've made no mention of one of the important attractions of options and futures trading: the way you are taxed on the profits. We won't go into the historical reasons why futures, and certain options, are taxed differently from everything else. Suffice it to say that Section 1256 of the Internal Revenue Code gives very special tax treatment to all futures contracts traded on the exchanges; and the broad index options are now treated also as "Section 1256 contracts."

When an investor buys or sells any of these contracts, no matter how long or short his or her holding period may be, the resulting gain or loss is taxed as 60% long-term capital gain or loss, and 40% short-term capital gain or loss. We repeat that this 60/40 gain or loss rule applies whether you have bought or sold (long or short), and whether the holding period is a day, 2 years, or any other period. Your gain is taxed at favorable rates even if the transaction has only lasted overnight. In mid-1985, the maximum federal tax bracket was 50%, and long-term capital gains were taxed at only 40% of ordinary rates, so that the maximum tax rate on long-term gains was 20%. Based on these rates, the maximum rate on a Section 1256 transaction worked out to 32%.

There's another twist, however: Your profit or loss is calculated and taxed as of the end of the year whether it is realized or unrealized. For tax purposes, every Section 1256 contract is *marked to market* at December 31—that is, it is treated as if it were sold on December 31 at the going market price. In the following year, you are taxed as if the contract had been newly bought or sold on December 31 at that price. This rule is intended to outlaw complicated transactions by which traders used to take their losses promptly for tax purposes, but postpone profits from year to year.

Section 1256 treatment applies, as we have said, to all exchange-traded futures contracts and to what are classified as *nonequity* options. Nonequity options include the major broad-based stock index options, debt options, commodity options and currency options.

And now you know another reason for the great popularity of trading in futures, index options, and interest rate options. If you make a profit, even overnight, Uncle Sam won't tax away more than 32% of it. It certainly beats working for a living.

However, options on the *narrow-based* stock indexes (specific industry indexes, etc.) are classified as *equity* options, together with all options on individual stocks. Equity options are taxed much like other securities, though special distinctions apply.

If you *buy* an equity option (put or call) and hold it 6 months or less, your gain or loss on selling it is short-term. If you hold it more than 6 months, your gain or loss is long-term. If you *write* an equity option (call or put), your gain or loss is short-term, irrespective of the length of the option term. If you *exercise* an individual stock option, various rules apply—consult your broker or accountant.

For at least 1985–86, a capital gain is long-term when the holding period reaches 6 months and a day. So it's possible to make a long-term gain on certain equity options, since the longer-term options run for as long as 9 months. This is a strategy worth considering, and we repeat that it applies to puts as well as calls.

17

AVOIDING DISASTER

Having just pointed out another of the advantages of options and futures (the tax advantage), we feel impelled to repeat some of the warnings we have given throughout this book about the dangers of these areas to inexperienced (and sometimes experienced) investors.

Set Rules

Because losses can develop so quickly in either options or futures, you should set careful rules for yourself before you begin.

If you are taking the speculative side, the amount you commit to options and/or futures trading should be an amount you can afford to lose completely—it may well happen.

Keep a Reserve

In buying an option, keep enough cash in reserve so that you can afford to renew the option for a subsequent period. Even if you have made an intelligent prediction, events in the markets may not develop as fast as you had hoped, and you don't want to be forced out of a position just when there may be a good chance of it going your way.

Don't be offended if your broker asks hard questions about your finances before letting you trade in options or futures. The broker is trying to protect you as well as the firm.

When to Get Out

If you find that you have lost as much as 50% of your original trading fund, consider getting out and thinking things over. Perhaps this kind of trading is not for you. For many people it's simply a mistake. And there are other, safer ways of investing.

Consider also the merits of getting out of each individual investment when the loss reaches 50%. Set clear objectives for each transaction: a target level at which you would get out and take your profit, and another level at which you would recognize a mistake and take your loss.

To make sure you follow out your own plans, consider entering *limit* orders with your broker in order to take a profit automatically at a certain level, and *stop loss* orders that will make you get out automatically when your losses reach a certain point. If you have a contract that is already profitable, set a stop loss order to limit the amount of the profit that can evaporate in the market. Your broker will be glad to help you with the details.

Beware of Pyramiding

Be particularly careful about *pyramiding*. In the futures markets, it's easy to use paper profits to build a larger position—sometimes a dangerously large one. Example: You buy a T-bond futures contract at 75, putting up margin of $2,500. The price rises to $77\frac{1}{2}$. You are ahead by $2,500 ($1,000 per point of gain) and still optimistic, so you use the additional $2,500 credit in your account to purchase an additional contract. But the price drops back to 75. Now, instead of being even, you are behind by $2,500. If the pyramiding had been allowed to go several more steps, the results could have been even worse. Don't let your commitments grow carelessly. The options and futures markets can be merciless.

18

SUMMING UP

Potentially profitable, potentially useful, potentially dangerous. All three phrases describe the options and futures arena. What should your approach be to these exciting but treacherous markets?

First, study the ways in which professional investors use options and futures for *protection*. We've explained how some of the mechanisms work for hedging risks. If any of these approaches fit your situation, don't hesitate to use them. The mark of an expert investor is often that he or she knows how to *limit risks*. If you can learn ways of limiting your risks for a reasonable price, you have made an important step toward long-run investment success.

The Importance of Being Skeptical

If you intend to speculate in these markets, stay careful, alert, and skeptical. Why skeptical? Because all sorts of nonsense is published by people who pretend that there are surefire ways of knowing which way the stock market will go, or which way interest rates will go. The most successful and knowledgeable professionals know that over short or intermediate periods, nothing in the world is harder than predicting the direction of the stock market or the debt markets.

Despite the lack of certainty, there are few things more exciting to study than the behavior of these markets. In the stock market, you can read works by both "fundamental" and "technical" analysts. The fundamental analysts rely on basic economic facts such as corporate profits, corporate balance sheets, industrial activity, etc. The technical analysts try to predict the movements of the stock market by studying the patterns and characteristics of the market itself, often with the aid of charts.

Both groups tend to have some triumphs and some defeats. The more you learn about both approaches, the better you will be able to understand and judge what the experts are saying. And the better will be your chances of finding one of those rare but profitable opportunities when you are right and the majority of the experts are wrong.

The interest rate field is equally fascinating. You can learn about the economics of interest rates, and the ways in which Federal Reserve policy influences interest rates. Here too, predictions are terribly difficult, but there are occasional opportunities when a cool-headed investor can speculate with reasonable odds and sometimes come up with exceptional results.

Going against the Crowd

Why do we talk about "occasional opportunities" and "rare opportunities"? Except for a few exceptionally gifted professionals, we don't know many people who can claim mastery of the week-to-week and month-to-month movements of the stock market and the interest rate markets. But there are occasional times when these markets are driven to extremes by waves of exaggerated optimism or pessimism. If you can keep your sense of proportion at such times, you may have a basis for successful speculating.

If you have the courage to buy stocks or bonds when everyone is panicking and prices are low, you may well be on the right track. And courage is sometimes needed to sell securities at times when prices are high and the experts assure you that everything is rosy.

At such times, options and futures can increase your profit potential enormously. Futures, of course, increase your leverage tremendously both ways—your potential for loss is likely to be just as great as your potential for profit. Options permit you nearly the same profit potential with limited risk, and may be your best choice when you expect a major turn in a market.

But if you use options, remember what we said in the previous chapter. Even if your prediction is right, your timing may be early. So keep enough cash in reserve so that you will be able to buy a second option if the market has failed to respond by the time the first option expires.

Thoughts on Individual Stock Options

In all the excitement about stock index options and interest rate options, we find that individual stock options are probably getting less attention than they used to. Which may be a mistake.

We've heard the opinion expressed that since it's hard to predict the direction of individual stocks, one might just as well play the whole market—via index options or index futures, for example. But some experts feel exactly the opposite.

It's instructive to listen to portfolio managers who have been successful in picking individual stocks. Many of them take the position that the general market is too irrational to predict, but that it's possible to select individual stocks successfully based on earnings, assets, management, and business prospects. (See *Understanding Common Stocks*.)

We don't intend here to probe into the art of stock selection, or *security analysis*. But it's an art that can be very profitable. And many amateurs who have worked at it have become successful at picking stocks and managing their own investments.

We pointed out that individual stock options don't enjoy the "60/40" tax treatment discussed in Chapter 16. But don't forget the other side of the coin. If you buy an individual stock option and hold it for more than 6 months, any gain on the sale is *all* long-term capital gain—taxed at only 40% of your regular tax rate.

There is often money to be made in markets where public interest is less and the opportunities are less carefully surveyed. To the extent that the crowd focuses on the newer stock index options, stock index futures, and interest rate options, there may be neglected opportunities in individual stock options. If you have strong convictions about a stock, buying the appropriate option can be a way of obtaining much greater leverage with a clearly defined risk. But be wary of options that don't trade actively, since you may have trouble getting in and out at a fair price.

Choices for Everyone

The options and futures markets offer variety, excitement, and great potential. All investments have risks and rewards, but in options and futures you see them at their most concentrated and most exciting. Are these markets for you? That's for you to decide. We hope we have made these incredible new marketplaces as exciting for you as they are for us.

GLOSSARY

American Stock Exchange (AMEX) The second leading
U.S. stock exchange, also a leader in option trading;
located in New York City.

AMEX Market Value Option A stock index option based on
an index of all stocks listed on the American Stock
Exchange.

Arbitrage A specialized type of trading based on price differentials. An arbitrageur purchases a security or commodity in one market planning to sell the same security or commodity in another market at a higher price;
or purchases one security or commodity while making
an offsetting sale of a different but related security or
commodity.

At-the-Money An option is at-the-money when the current
market value of the underlying stock or index exactly
equals the exercise price of the option. See Chapter 6.

Bear An investor who expects the stock market (or a particular stock) to go down.

Bull An investor who expects the stock market (or a particular stock) to go up.

Call An option to buy.

Cash Secured Put A put written by an investor, when the
investor has deposited sufficient cash with the broker to
cover the full exercise price of the put.

CD (Certificate of Deposit) A "time deposit" in a bank, ma-
turing on a specific date and traditionally evidenced by
a certificate.

Closing Transaction An option transaction that eliminates
a previously existing long or short position in the
option.

Covered Call A call option written by someone who owns
the underlying security.

Dow Jones Industrial Average ("Dow") See Chapter 11.

Equity Options For tax purposes, equity options include all
options on individual stocks and on the narrow-based
stock indexes. See Chapter 16.

Exercise Price The price at which the holder of an option
has the right to buy or sell the underlying security.

Expiration Date The latest date for exercising an option at
the Options Clearing Corporation.

Futures See Chapter 3.

Futures Options   See Chapter 14.

GNMA or "Ginnie Mae"   The Government National Mortgage Association, a quasi-governmental agency carrying the full faith and credit of the U.S. government, which purchases mortgages from the original mortgage lenders.

Hedge, Hedger   To hedge is to take an investment position that reduces or eliminates the risk in another investment position. A hedger is one who hedges. See Chapter 9.

In-the-Money   An option is in-the-money when it has some positive intrinsic value based on the current market value of the underlying security or index. See Chapter 6.

Index Call   A call option based on a stock market index.

Index Future   A futures contract based on a stock market index.

Index Option   An option based on a stock market index.

Intrinsic Value   The value of an option if immediately exercised. See Chapter 6.

Leverage   A multiplication effect that increases potential profit or loss, as when a large asset is controlled by a relatively small investment, through borrowing or otherwise.

Limit Order   A trading order that authorizes a purchase only if the price dips to a specified level, or a sale only if the price rises to a specified level.

Liquid Investment   An investment that can be converted easily into cash, without penalty.

Long   In the securities industry, you are long a security when you own it.

Major Market Index   A stock market index constructed similarly to the Dow Jones Industrial Average. See Chapter 11.

Margin   Buying a stock or bond on margin means that part of the purchase price is borrowed from a broker; the margin is the amount the customer puts up. In futures, the margin is not part of the purchase price, but a good faith deposit.

Margin Call   The demand by a broker for additional cash or securities to fund a margin account when your equity in the account declines near the minimum allowed by the firm.

Mark to Market   To recalculate the value of an account based on latest market prices.

Market Price   The latest price of a security (or other asset) in the market where the security (or other asset) is traded.

Multiplier   The dollar value of a stock index option contract is the value of the index times an arbitrary multiplier (usually 100).

NYSE Composite Index   See Chapter 11.

Naked Call   See Uncovered Call.

New York Stock Exchange (NYSE)   The leading stock exchange in the U.S. (and the world).

Nonequity Options   For tax purposes, nonequity options include the major broad-based stock index options, debt options, commodity options, and currency options. See Chapter 16.

Option   The right to buy or sell a specific security or other asset at a predetermined price for a given period of time.

Options Clearing Corporation (OCC)   An organization formed by the various options exchanges which clears, coordinates, and in effect guarantees the fulfillment of all options traded on the exchanges.

Out-of-the-Money   An option is out-of-the-money when it has no present intrinsic value, based on the current market value of the underlying security or index. See Chapter 6.

Paper Gain (Loss)   See Unrealized Gain (Loss).

Premium   The price paid for an option, or the market price of an option.

Put   An option to sell.

Pyramiding   In futures trading, using paper profits to purchase additional futures contracts (a potentially dangerous procedure).

Realized Gain (Loss)   The actual gain or loss on sale of a security or other asset.

Short   In the securities industry, you are short a security when you owe it to someone, but don't own it. (If you also own it, you are said to be both long and short.)

Spread   See Chapter 7.

Standard & Poor's 100 (S&P 100)   See Chapter 11.

Standard & Poor's 500 (S&P 500)   See Chapter 11.

Stock Index Option   An option based on a stock market index.

Stop Order, Stop Loss Order   A type of trading order usually used to protect a profit or limit a loss. A stop order in a particular security becomes a market order when the market price of the security reaches or sells through a specified stop price.

Straddle   See Chapter 7.

Striking Price   The exercise price of an option.

Time Value   The speculative value of an option in the market, over and above its intrinsic value. See Chapter 6.

Treasury Bill (T-bill)   A short-term debt security of the U.S. Treasury, issued with a maturity of 3, 6 or 12 months and sold on a discounted basis.

Treasury Bond (T-bond)   A U.S. Treasury debt security with an original maturity of more than 10 years from the date of issuance.

Uncovered Call   A call option written by someone who does not own the underlying security.

Unrealized Gain (Loss)   On a security or other asset that you still own, the gain or loss you would realize if it were sold at current market value. You have an unrealized gain if the current market price is above your cost, an unrealized loss if the current market price is below your cost.

Value Line Index   See Chapter 11.

Writing Calls, Writer of Calls   See Chapter 7.

ABOUT THE AUTHORS

ARNOLD CORRIGAN, noted financial expert, is the author of *How Your IRA Can Make You A Millionaire* and is a frequent guest on financial talk shows. A senior officer of a large New York investment advisory firm, he holds Bachelor's and Master's degrees in economics from Harvard and has written for *Barron's* and other financial publications.

PHYLLIS C. KAUFMAN, the originator of *The No-Nonsense Guides*, has made her mark in a number of fields. She is a Philadelphia entertainment attorney, theatrical producer, marketing consultant and former dancer. She holds degrees from Brandeis and Temple Universities and is listed in *Who's Who in American Law*.

NOTES

NOTES

NOTES